CHARACTER ARCS

Fiction by Jordan McCollum

Spy Another Day novels
I, Spy
Spy for a Spy
Tomorrow We Spy

Spy Another Day Prequels
Spy Noon (novella)
Mr. Nice Spy (novella)
Spy by Night (novel)

Nonfiction by Jordan McCollum

Character Sympathy:
Creating characters your readers <u>have</u> to root for

WRITING CRAFT SERIES

CHARACTER ARCS

founding, forming and finishing
your character's internal journey

JORDAN McCOLLUM

FOREWORD by JANICE HARDY

DURHAM CREST BOOKS

CHARACTER ARCS © 2013 Jordan McCollum

First printing, 2013

Published by Durham Crest Books
Pleasant Grove, Utah
Set in Linux Libertine

ISBN 978-1-940096-05-6

PRINTED IN THE UNITED STATES OF AMERICA

For everyone who has ever taught me,
inside or outside a classroom.

Contents

CHAPTER 3

CHAPTER 4

CHAPTER 5

CHAPTER 6

FOREWORD

Character arcs are the heart of a story, often pushing the characters to get up and keep moving when all is lost. They're the personal journeys that help characters win what matters most to them, and become the people they always dreamed they could be, the reason readers care about what happens to those characters.

From a technical standpoint, character arcs provide the motivation for why the heroes struggle, why they sacrifice, and why they do all those things the plot says they should do. They provide the emotional fuel of the book, working together to craft a story that grabs readers and doesn't let go.

Seeing a character you love struggle to overcome problems and become a better person by the end of the story is one of the best aspects about reading a book. That struggle entertains us as readers, makes us worry about the character, and maybe even inspires us to be better people as well.

Such is the power of a character arc.

Jordan McCollum will show you how to access that power in your own work.

She'll show you how to craft character arcs that answer the critical question "Why does this story matter?" and use those arcs to deepen your novel. She'll show you how to put those character arcs into action and bring your characters to life.

She'll even show you where in your novel key elements of a character arc can have the most impact.

Sometimes the struggle to write a compelling character arc is just as grueling as what we put our characters through. Emotional journeys, hidden hurts, lies believed and truths avoided can be so simple to create, yet be so difficult to weave successfully into a carefully constructed plot. Trying to figure out when (and where) to have a character realize a flaw or learn a valuable lesson can leave you banging your head against the keyboard for days.

But it just got a lot easier. This book will ease your struggle, and help you make your characters' struggles harder and more poignant.

Plots may entertain, but without a character to care about, a story falls flat. The character arc is what turns that flat plot into a story worth reading—and worth telling. A well-crafted character arc resonates with readers long after the last page is turned.

And Jordan McCollum will show you how to do just that.

Janice Hardy,
Author of The Healing Wars Trilogy

INTRODUCTION

WHY CHARACTER ARCS MATTER

In the course of most works of fiction, the major characters don't just experience the events of the plot—the plot changes them. They learn and grow, ultimately succeeding at the climax of the story because of all they've gained.

This internal journey is sometimes called an internal plot, emotional plot, emotional journey, or character arc. No matter what name you use, that arc is vital in most fiction to connect with your readers on an emotional level. Even the greatest plot in the world can ring flat if the character's internal journey isn't dramatic enough. For a character to truly resonate with readers, he should change and grow over the course of the story.

A character who doesn't arc (with specific exceptions) isn't nearly as fulfilling to read about. In *Save the Cat! The Last Book on Screenwriting You'll Ever Need*, Blake Snyder describes character arcs (italics in original):

> *Arc* is a term that means "the change that occurs to any character from the beginning, through the middle, and to the end of each character's 'journey.'" . . . But when it's done well, when we can chart the growth and change each character undergoes in the course of a movie [or novel], it's a poem. What you are saying in essence is: This story, this experience, is so important,

> so life-changing for all involved—even you, the audience—it affects every single person that is in its orbit. From time immemorial, all good stories show growth and track change in all its [*sic*] characters.
>
> Why is this?
>
> I think the reason that characters must change in the course of a movie [or novel] is because if your story is worth telling, it must be vitally important to everyone involved. This is why set-ups and payoffs for each character have to be crafted carefully and tracked throughout. (135)

Character arcs aren't just nice for readers—these arcs show that the events of our story are worth reading about. The character arc demonstrates the story's impact, an answer to the reader's subconscious question, "Why does this story matter?"

Answer that question, and your fiction will feel like more than just a pleasurable way to pass some free time.

This book covers discovering your character's arc, implementing it in your story, and using the arc to best effect. This book is aimed at writers with a good grasp of storytelling, story structure, and mechanics who are looking to elevate their stories and make their characters more powerful. Far from a write-by-numbers manual, this approach examines the basic mechanics of character change to show many ways to apply this principle in your own work, with numerous examples.

ABOUT THE EXAMPLES IN THIS BOOK

I use many examples in this book because the concepts of building a character arc can range into the theoretical, making them harder to apply to our own fiction. I've found in teaching this topic online and in person that multiple examples are sometimes necessary to help clarify or illustrate a principle. Several sections use more than one example to a illustrate specific point to show the myriad ways an idea can be put into action.

A few examples are used in several places throughout the book:

- *Too Shy to Spy*, a nonexistent novel used throughout the chapters on discovering your character's arc and putting your character's arc into action, to demonstrate how to develop and implement a character arc.
- *Bloodstone*, a completed, forthcoming novel I wrote, referenced in the chapters on discovering your character's arc and in the section on tailoring the antagonist, and further developed in the chapter on arcs in relationship stories.

While there are many examples throughout this work from movies, plays, and books, both classic and contemporary, most of the shorter examples are invented for the purposes of illustrating the specific principle in the section, or drawn from my own work. I use my own works not in an effort to promote those books, but because as the author, I can comment on what went into the development of those characters' arcs. I can only comment on the execution of other authors' character arcs.

A full list of the examples used in this book appears in the References section.

Discovering Your Character's Arc

Whether you're in the idea phase
or you've completed your story,
these techniques help you find
the best way for your character
to grow throughout the story.

Like good stories, good character arcs seldom happen by chance, or on the first try. When I first began writing, I didn't give much thought to character arcs. If they got in there, it was either a coincidence or something I added in revisions. After that, about the time I wrote a series of blog posts on this topic, I figured out my characters' arcs halfway through a first draft, and I often stopped to go back and adjust what I had. Now that I've gained a better understanding of how character arcs work and how to execute them, I contemplate the character's arc more before I start drafting.

Whether you plan from the beginning, figure it out along the way, or add it all in edits, there's no wrong way to implement a character arc.

If you don't already have a journey for your character in mind, this chapter explores ways to find your character's internal journey, no matter how much or how little you've worked on the character and his external story.

FROM STARTING AND ENDING POINTS

Every character, and every character arc, has to start somewhere. We know that in the ordinary world at the outset of the story, something is wrong. That doesn't just mean a love interest or a murderer that needs to be brought to justice—there's something is missing from the protagonist's life, something deeper that the character needs on an emotional level.

Screenwriter Michael Hauge refers to this as the character's longing or need. In his terminology, a longing is a desire the character is aware of and could even obtain, if the character would only act (but he doesn't). A need is subconscious, something he lacks but isn't aware of, which will improve his life. It's the missing piece of his existence, and whether he realizes it or not, he will never be fully happy without it. Either of these can make a suitable character arc, though if done well, the subconscious need can be more compelling because the whole journey of change is generally more dramatic.

The character's subconscious need can take many forms. It could be love or justice—or it could be forgiveness, healing, resolve, courage, wisdom, etc. If you're familiar with the Hero's Journey, the archetypal journey of a fictional hero, you'll recall that at the end of the story, the hero returns a changed man because he now has "the elixir." In the Hero's Journey terminology, a major part of that "elixir" is the fulfillment of this subconscious need or conscious longing, this internal journey, the process of fixing what's wrong in his life. This is what the character gains in the end, what the story events mean to him, how the events change him forever.

To use this method of discovering your character's arc, take a look at the state your character is in at the beginning or end of your novel. If you already know the flaw at the beginning, you can look for ways to "fix" it through the story events. If you know what lesson the character will end up learning, you can set her up in the opposite place.

If the character will find love, she starts off lonely—or better still, subconsciously in need of love, or a better love match. If she needs healing, she starts off damaged. Conversely, if the character starts off dissolute, he can develop resolve through-

2

out the story. If he's afraid, he learns to find courage; if she's naïve, she can learn wisdom.

The character's end point is a good guide, too. We know that the character ends up victorious in some way, going from denigrated to vindicated. But the internal journey has to dig deeper. What does he *learn*? How does she *change* to accomplish her goal? Identifying these emotional ending points also helps us to set up the character in the opposite place at the outset.

Developmental examples

Let's say we start off with a hero who can't get a date because he lacks confidence. Obviously, we want to help him gain self-assurance throughout the events of the story. We can—we must!—engineer those events to help him become confident. (We'll be coming back to this example, so let's call this story *Too Shy to Spy*.)

Starting with what the character gains in the end is a little more involved. Let's say in the conclusion of our book, our hero ends up being recognized by the medical establishment for his revolutionary new procedure. This external event can help us figure out the internal journey as well. What does the character *discover* about himself and the world? How does he change to accomplish his goal? Perhaps he too gains confidence. (If so, maybe he doesn't need the AMA's stamp of approval to know he's a fantastic doctor.) Or maybe his arc is to learn to accept help, or to not chase the limelight, gaining humility or modesty.

Then all we have to do is set him up in the opposite position. If

3

he gains confidence, he'll start off constantly seeking others' approval, worrying over their opinions, thinking little of himself. On the other hand, if we'd rather explore a character journey of humility instead, he'll start off more arrogant, believing he doesn't need any help or that he's above his colleagues and friends. If he learns not to chase the limelight, he might start off seeking fame—maybe dating a socialite just for the visibility, etc.

When you have so many choices, how can you figure out which works best? Weigh them out. Does one speak to you more—or better still, seem to match your character better? Does one inspire more or better ideas for external plot events?

Those external plot events are another good source to look for character arcs.

FROM THE PLOT

Perhaps you have a good idea what will happen in the course of the story, but you aren't sure how the events of the plot will affect the character—perhaps you're not even sure *who* the character is.

Plot and character are so often intertwined that it's difficult to flesh out one without the other. When I start with an initial idea about the plot events for a story, I usually have to figure out more about the character before I can move forward on the plot. To do this, I try to think of the worst or strangest person to put in this plot situation, someone who would inherently bring a lot of conflict. For example, you might start with the idea of some sort of bodyguard assigned to protect a woman who secretly needed no protection—because she was a spy herself (and, in fact, was targeting her bodyguard and/or his country). From there, you can look for an event which would have the hero assigned to protect her. Let's use an attempt on her life. Then we can brainstorm the worst, most devastating person to be targeting her, perhaps her beloved father.

Once we have the basics of the plot and its most suitable characters figured out, we can turn to building the characters and their arcs. In our current example, we must now determine the setting, what kind of person would have become a spy in that setting, what her personality would be like, etc.

At the same time, we should contemplate how the plot events might change the character. Again in this example, we might ponder how the heroine would feel after discovering her father's betrayal and how she could dig deep for a source of inner strength to act from that point. What state does she start in? How does she change throughout the story? How does her father's betrayal affect her life's trajectory?

This seems to be the method I use most often for figuring out my character arcs. I'm usually inspired by plot ideas. Contemplating the characters' journeys helps to ensure that my characters aren't whipped around by the plot's whims. Instead, they're acting toward not only the external plot's purposes but also their internal motivations.

Developmental example

Say we have a plot: a quest for a hidden treasure with religious ties. We need a character to have an arc. Perhaps our character is actually searching for the treasure to prove that it doesn't exist and the adherents of this hokey religion are all wasting their lives.

Again, there could be many characters and internal journeys here. An obvious arc would have him starting in a position of doubt, and he could come to find faith. Or maybe he hates this hokey religion because of a bad experience with a member of the faith, so he's trying to exact revenge—and then he can journey to finding justice (though probably not in the way he thinks).

That internal journey just doesn't grab me. Since we're still in the development phase, we can reconceptualize the character now. What kind of character might be looking for this treasure? Maybe instead of a doubter, a believer would work better. That could be an integral part of his character: he *believes*, even though everyone around him doubts and ridicules his archaeological theory.

However, having someone else come to believe him is very external. He believes despite everyone's ridicule, so he's definitely not seeking approval, and a journey to discover he doesn't need that approval wouldn't be as compelling. Perhaps instead, he should come to realize he does need help. He's used to rejecting (or even pre-rejecting) people around him because they ridicule his theory, so he wants to go it alone. When someone finally believes in him, it's hard for him to accept help, but he ultimately learns he can't do everything by himself.

This is the method and journey I used in a forthcoming novel,

Bloodstone. We'll be returning to this example as well.

FROM THE CHARACTER

Of course, the above methods work great if you already know your plot (if you're at the end of planning, in drafting or in revisions). If your character is inspiring the story, but you don't know her well yet, you probably don't know how she's going to grow—or perhaps even very much about her yet. Still, there should be one thing you know about your character at this phase: what motivates her.

That might sound a little deep, especially when we've just said that you don't know your character well yet. But as we dig into whatever you do already know about him, you can use that information to extrapolate deeper motivations, longings and needs.

Some good places to start this "character archaeology" are by looking at the aspects of the character you do know, including his:
- Strengths
- Profession
- Hobbies
- Reason for going on the external journey
- Prized possessions or people
- Life goals

Once you've identified a few of these, start digging deeper with every writer's favorite question: "Why?" Why did she decide to become a ballet dancer? Why did he take up ferroequinology? Why did she decide to investigate her neighbor's murder? Why does she love her best friend/mother so much?

"How?" is also a good question, especially focusing on the character's emotional response or reasoning. How does restoring an old house affect her emotionally? How does his strength, his intelligence, make him act? How is she pursuing her life goals now, and is that effective?

These questions help us dig deeper to discover the character's core motivations. Maybe she wants to restore an old house because she never had a stable home as a child and she wants to create one now. Or maybe she loves history and sees this as her way of contributing to and preserving her area's heritage. Maybe both!

Nailing down the character's core motivations can help us discover what she's lacking, too. Often, turning to these favorite questions helps us dig even deeper. If our heroine is working on restoring that old house to create a real home and preserve the area's heritage, why? What does she get from doing this, on an emotional level? What does she *need?*

Similarly, we can take one of these aspects that might be a positive thing and extrapolate it to find a negative extreme. If our hero's great strength is his intelligence, perhaps he doesn't suffer fools well. If our heroine excels at keeping confidences, maybe she's also really good at keeping secrets from people who should know them, or she's very bad at trusting other people with her own.

Developmental examples

Our hero might be a great listener. Everyone turns to him with problems, and he always has a sympathetic ear. He will drop anything to be there for a friend. How can that strength be a weakness? Perhaps he doesn't know how to say no. He may become burdened with too much information. Someone could misinterpret his friendship as a more romantic interest. Maybe he needs to learn how to have boundaries.

In my novel *I, Spy*, I started off with a plot idea, but I knew I needed the main character to be a CIA operative. To come up with her character arc, I contemplated what kind of person becomes a spy, and why she wouldn't tell her boyfriend about her real job, and what she would learn throughout the story. Eventually, I found I needed her to believe, mistakenly, that she's better off alone. From there, I constructed her backstory: a family history filled with divorces. (I also looked for events in the plot to reinforce this belief: a coworker whose pre-occupation with his family puts her in danger.)

For another example, let's say we know our heroine lost her job some time ago. She goes on the story journey because (through story events which we're engineering) she is very specifically led to believe that this journey will give her life financial stability. So, at the beginning, she's not doing well financially.

But if we dig deeper, it's not just that she wants more money. Serious financial need creates a lot of problems, but we might boil down the issue to one of instability. She may not be sure where her next meal is coming from, or whether she'll have electricity or be evicted soon. How does that instability affect the character emotionally? Naturally, she's afraid. The external journey may be her quest for cash, but the internal character arc will be her quest to allay her fears.

Match that up with an external plot with an external goal that aligns with an external manifestation of those fears. With our unemployed heroine, we might give her an external goal that matches with the external manifestation of her need: money. She might go on a reality TV game show for the prize.

This external goal, however, doesn't meet her *internal* needs. What do you want to bet a cash prize won't guarantee her a perfectly stable life? You could tell a story about a woman who wants external financial stability above all else, and then she gets it, but her internal growth isn't going to be very deep if we never scratch the surface of her underlying emotional weakness.

Instead, if we realize that the desire for stability is a manifestation of underlying fear, we can use the events of the story to help her (or force her) to gain the courage she needs to press forward in an uncertain world, regardless of whether she wins the jackpot.

READY TO ROLL

Once you've determined your character's internal and external journeys—at least in general terms—we're ready to put that arc into action in the story itself.

PUTTING YOUR CHARACTER'S ARC INTO ACTION

Once we have the character's trajectory,
we're ready to start weaving it
with the events of the external plot.

EXTERNAL EVENTS, INTERNAL GROWTH

Internal growth typically doesn't happen spontaneously, at least not in fiction. People, even fictional people, don't change unless they're forced to—usually by the events of the plot and the world around them.

I love how RITA-winning author and editor Alicia Rasley puts it in her article "Changes and Choices: External Action and Internal Reaction":

> Character-driven fiction is about internal change. Paradoxically, external action is usually needed to bring on this change. External action is the surest catalyst for both internal growth and reader interest. Sure, your protagonist could overcome his distaste for intimacy and his dread of family by going to a psychologist twice a week for ten years . . . but who wants to read about that? Even psychologists, probably, would put down a novel about therapy sessions to pick up a novel about a woman who learns to trust by being blackmailed into joining a secret team to rescue the kidnapped clone of Thomas Edison.

As important as the emotional, mental and attitudinal changes of the internal journey are, they don't happen in isolation.

Because these changes mark internal growth, it's important to select a character arc that represents a true internal change: something the character can change about himself or herself. For example, a character journey where the character wins over the respect of someone else doesn't represent an internal change: it's a change in someone else, and something that most fictional characters (just like real people) don't have ultimate control over, no matter how much they strive to influence it.

For an internal journey, the character should focus on what he can ultimately control: his own motivations, reactions and attitudes. Instead of striving to win others' respect, perhaps the character's journey is finding his own self-worth—or coming to realize that others' opinions of him don't matter.

The external events of the plot are necessary to prompt the character's internal growth, but an external goal for the character arc usually isn't sufficient to show the character himself growing and changing.

FOUNDING: THE BEGINNING

We've got a rough idea for beginning of the character's journey. Now we need to establish the starting point for maximum effect. To do this, we need an "illustrating event" that shows the "before" picture of emotional state, and demonstrates how bad that emotional state is for our character.

Showing the broken beginning

One of the first aphorisms we learn in writing fiction is *Show, don't tell.* The same general principle is a good guideline for the character's internal journey as well.

Showing the character's internal state is especially important because it's the only way the reader can really understand and believe that the starting point is a problem for the character, and that the ending point is a solution. The narrator cannot just inform the reader, "HERO HAS THIS PROBLEM." Other characters cannot just inform the reader, "HERO HAS THIS PROBLEM." For a reader to believe, to understand the depth of the problem, to recognize how much the character *needs* this change, the reader must see the problem in action.

If the character is looking for stability (because he's afraid), readers must *see* that fear dominating his life. He decides not to do something he really wanted to because of his fears, for example. If the character is too outspoken, we should show how it's hurting him, such as through losing friends or alienating loved ones.

So, how do we use this storytelling theory in our work? First we need an opportunity to *show* the character's starting point in action: an "illustrating event." Brainstorm situations where the character would react in his pre-arc way:

- A character who learns wisdom would be naïve at the outset, so we need an opportunity to show his naïveté. Maybe he rushes to do something a wiser person wouldn't. Maybe he behaves rashly. Maybe he judges someone else too soon.

- A character who learns courage would be ruled by his fears at the outset. Sometimes this is harder to show, but perhaps you can give the character an opportunity to do something they've always wanted to do: start a restaurant, go skydiving, pursue an attractive individual. Have the character consider that option, even want it—but ultimately, his fears

15

win, and he second-guesses himself out of acting.

Screenwriter Michael Hauge has a great model for creating and showing this broken beginning. The character has some sort of "wound" in her backstory, often an external, painful event. We don't have to see this event in the story, but we will see its aftereffects, because this wound very much shapes the character's belief about herself and the world. This mistaken belief often takes the shape of fear. It leads the character to assume a "mask," a false way she presents herself to the world to protect herself or cover these fears. The mask isn't the real character, though. Her true "essence" is who she really is or wants to be(come) despite her mistaken belief.

Hauge's example is *Shrek*. His wound is that people have always run from him, so he believes he must be terrifying. This fear of rejection makes him assume a mask of a big, scary ogre to keep others at a distance and protect himself from experiencing rejection. But his true essence is someone who *does* want and need those connections—friends, love.

One word of caution here: Make sure your character is still worthy of sympathy! The weakness can work in your favor—it can help to increase character sympathy. Or it can backfire if the weakness is a particularly appalling attitude or behavior, or if the character shows no other strengths, such as courage, will, backbone, spunk, humor, etc.

Making the emotional starting point bad

We already know that something in the protagonist's life is amiss. This problem has to be bad enough that the character

16

must fix it—or she must be compelled to fix it—now. The character has probably already learned to cope with this long-standing attitude or neurosis. The more ingrained the attitude or behavior is, the harder it will be to change (and the more compelling it will be to read).

External events, the plot, need to show that the character's starting point won't work anymore, demonstrating the untenable situation to not just the reader, but to the character, too. Again, even fictional people don't change unless they're forced to!

If you haven't plotted out your character arcs in advance (or even if you have), the beginning of the character arc often needs the most work. We have to make the change as dramatic as possible, matching and offsetting the ending. Or, turning to *Save the Cat!* by Blake Snyder again, we must use the "Take a Step Back" principle:

> Take a Step Back applies to all your characters. In order to show how everyone grows and changes in the course of your story, you must take them all back to the starting point. Don't get caught up in the end result and deny us the fun of how they get there. We want to see it happen. To everyone.
>
> This is just one more example of how movies [and novels] must show the audience everything: all the change, all the growth, all the action of a hero's journey. By taking it all back as far as possible, by drawing the bow back to its very quivering end point, the flight of the arrow is its strongest, longest and best. The Take a Step Back rule double-checks this.

> If you feel like your story or any of its characters isn't showing us the entire flight, the entire journey... Take a Step Back and show it all to us. We want to see it. (156)

Dig deeper in the beginning and show a big change! If your hero learns to show appreciation to his wife in the course of the story, don't just have him work late a couple times or forget their anniversary. I'm reminded of the beginning of the movie *True Lies.* (How could we have a book on character arcs without mentioning Arnold Schwarzenegger?) Both the hero and the heroine aren't just complacent in their marriage. They don't communicate beyond small talk, their physical relationship is nonexistent and the hero misses the birthday celebration his wife and daughter planned for him. They're not on the verge of divorce, but what they have isn't much of a marriage or a family.

The problem may appear small enough for the hero to ignore or handle easily at the very beginning, but we need to take it a step back, possibly developing the character's bad situation throughout the opening chapters.

So, how do we show the emotional starting point is bad? When we're showing the character's emotional beginning, we need to make sure there are negative consequences to the pre-arc behavior pattern. A character who shows naïveté by rushing in or behaving rashly will reap bad results. Her foolish actions should cause some sort of trouble for her.

With a character who is ruled by his fears, the reader needs to see that living under the thumb of his own fears doesn't give him the life he truly wants. For example, for our shy, unconfident hero in *Too Shy to Spy*, if he sees a beautiful woman and considers asking her out, but is ultimately too afraid to, we could have the object of his affections be completely ignorant of his intent. However, I think it's more compelling if she shows some small level of interest in him, even just as friends. When he fails to ask her out, then she begins to withdraw—or someone else swoops in and snaps her up.

For the ultimate impact, time these events close enough together to imply a causal relationship. Perhaps the hero and the woman are talking, and he's considering asking her out. But the moment he lets his fears get in the way, and he decides *not* to ask her out, *then* someone else is able to interrupt their conversation and the interloper succeeds in asking her out.

Empirically speaking, there may be no direct cause-and-effect between these events. The woman and the other man can't read the hero's mind to know he's chickening out. However, presenting the story actions as if they're a stimulus and response chain cements that idea in the minds of our readers and characters alike.

Now the readers know how bad the emotional beginning is because they've seen the starting point in action in the illustrating event and its negative consequences.

THE IMPETUS FOR ACTION

Whatever illustrating event and negative consequences we use can serve as an isolated incident, or as an impetus to the larger plot. Both are equally valid story structures.

When the illustrating event is a direct impetus to the plot, this illustrating incident helps the character to act in some way directly related to that event: their reaction to that incident is part of the chain of external events running through the story. Unless your story is very short, the character's reaction will not resolve the underlying problem with a complete, perfect, 180-degree turn. The reaction may not even address the problem.

If we're using this method, after the hero of *Too Shy to Spy* fails to ask his crush out, maybe he tries to win her affections as a secret admirer. He sends her notes and gifts and flowers, but she thinks they're from someone else. Slowly, he becomes bolder with his gifts and with his actions, until he has gained the courage to take the final risk and ask her out—made most brave because he really isn't sure what she'll answer. If we were using this plot for our book, we'd probably want to title it something else—unless, of course, we managed to intertwine this romance plot and the mistaken identity/spy plot.

On the other hand, if the illustrating event is an isolated incident, it can be useful in establishing the "ordinary world" of the story, the place where the character has lived and operated with this coping mechanism for some time. The coping mechanism, however, is causing more and more problems.

When using the isolated incident as a story starter, it's generally best to begin with a moment of change. Perhaps this is the eighth time the hero of *Too Shy to Spy* has tried to ask out this attractive woman. He really wants to go out with her, and she's receptive to it, but he's too afraid. So why are we using the eighth event as the starting point for the story? This event should mark a moment of change, when the character must try something different. Failure #8 constitutes the moment of change because after he fails, he decides to finally go out and do something about it.

So how does he change—and how does that get our "real" story started? Maybe he decides the clothes make the man, so he needs some designer duds. As he heads out of the department store, he's mistaken for an international man of mystery, and gets dragged into a multinational plot which will force him to face his fears. Naturally, at the end, he'll return triumphant and confident, and finally ask the object of his affections on a date.

Note how directly the plot was tied to the illustrating incident when we use that event to start the plot. The illustrating incident in the first example was a romantic failure, which precipitated a romance plot. When we use an isolated event for the illustrating incident, as in the second option, the plot may go in a very different direction. It's wise, if possible, to make sure we don't jar our readers. If someone started *Too Shy to Spy* expecting a romance and got a spy novel, the reader wouldn't be very happy. Even if the illustrating event doesn't directly start the external plot, we need to see that external plot or its genre foreshadowed in the opening somehow.

No matter which plot we use for *Too Shy to Spy*, the biggest enemy of a shy hero is typically himself, even if he has a rival for her affections. His own weaknesses and fears are the biggest obstacle to his success and happiness. But in stories with an external antagonist, we can also carefully design the antagonist of the story to illustrate the protagonist's emotional journey.

TAILORING THE ANTAGONIST

For the most effective character arc in stories with an external antagonist, we need to see that antagonist working against the character's internal journey as well as the external journey (the plot).

Just like the broken beginning might not be a conscious problem for the protagonist—she does, after all, cope with these fears or problems, and she has for a while—the antagonist's internal attack might be more psychological, especially when the antagonist either shares or reflects the protagonist's weakness.

Antagonist as reflection

One way to do this is to align the antagonist with the main character's fear, this mistaken belief, this problem shown in the emotional starting point. Throughout the story, the antagonist illustrates the ultimate fate of someone who never solves the problem the protagonist is facing.

If the heroine's weakness is a lack of trust, perhaps the perfect antagonist for her has that same weakness, an inability to trust. In some way, that should be his downfall. Maybe he can't delegate some task to his minions, he has to do it all himself, but he just physically can't. His inability to grow sets him up for a defeat by the heroine who has learned that lesson (and, naturally, will also be relying on the friends she's learned to trust to help overwhelm the antagonist).

In my forthcoming novel *Bloodstone*, I tried several arcs for the characters, including the antagonist. Ultimately, I think the best, most convincing arc for the antagonist begins with him sharing a weakness with the heroine: a lack of belief. His arc shows him regaining belief, but at the critical climax moment, his belief again fails, showing his change isn't authentic. He's left bitterer than ever, lashing out at the main characters. His moral faltering at the key moment means the main characters, who *have* learned their lessons, can become stronger than him and defeat him.

Conversely, the antagonist might also show the same trait as the protagonist, but presented as a strength.

Antagonist as opposite + foil as reflection

Another way to do this is to give the antagonist the exact opposite strength of the protagonist's weakness. Screenwriter Michael Hauge also addresses this in his book *Writing Screenplays that Sell.* He suggests also using a foil character or, in his terminology, the reflection, "the character who most supports the hero's outer motivation or is in the same basic situation" (73). Often this is a friend of the protagonist, with the same weakness taken to an extreme. The hero is able to see the negative effects of both extreme examples, and learn to synthesize a happy medium to successfully move forward while both the antagonist and the foil cannot.

To put it in more concrete terms, let's use a character journey of learning to balance family and work. The hero has a good friend from work, a foil character, who is *too* involved with his family. Not only do they distract from his work, bring down his performance, and ultimately cripple him emotionally, they also

23

manipulate and use him. The foil character allows all this to happen, perhaps even enabling his crazy family. The hero may start out in similar straits.

Meanwhile, our antagonist, their boss, is only out for himself. Not having a family, the boss continually penalizes the hero for ever putting his family before work. The foil character, naturally, gets even more punishment.

In the end, in Hauge's storytelling structure, the protagonist must recognize how he is *like* the antagonist, and *unlike* the foil in order to grow. While the antagonist and/or foil character may change throughout the story, neither of them is able to learn from his mistakes (as we might call them in this paradigm) to become a better, stronger person.

The hero in this example sees how he's *like* the antagonist—capable of performing at work, able to compete in the workplace. He also recognizes how he's *not* like the foil—he values his family, but he cannot let them rule his life any more than he'll let his boss railroad him.

By moderating the antagonist's strength and the foil character's weakness, the protagonist comes to a synthesis, successfully combining these lessons to grow to a healthier state emotionally. Both the antagonist and the foil character end up with outcomes that are far less ideal: the foil is henpecked and demoted, while the antagonist may be successful at work, yet very much alone. The hero has both success at work and a happy, healthy family relationship.

This dual counterexample method is perhaps most effective for a character journey with a very finely nuanced end point, learning some lesson about moderation.

But before we come to that ultimate conclusion, we need to prepare our character by learning those lessons throughout the middle. Now that we've established our character's journey, shown the bad starting point, and started our character on the path, the character arc will help us avoid the sagging middle.

FORMING: THE MIDDLE

We've embarked on our story's internal journey. Now what? In the middle of the book, we need to show the character's gradual growth by failing over and over again. Doesn't that sound pleasant?

How do we need to make our characters fail? We won't just trap them inside their heads—we need to turn to external action to force that internal change.

Using external action

Again, external action is the best way to both illustrate and force internal growth. As a handy bonus, it also helps keep your readers interested.

As you're designing your plot and your character arc, try to narrow your focus to plot events that will force your character to confront the central issue of the character arc. To make sure that the external action is prompting your internal changes, author/editor Alicia Rasley suggests linking the external events and internal arc in stimulus-response units. Look at both your story and your character journey to come up with these, and then see how the external events can be a stimulus for the "right" internal response at that phase.

This method allows gradual change which *shows* the journey better than thinking or pontificating about it could. The progressive approach also creates a great opportunity to show the character's resistance and reluctance, making the final choice even more satisfying and compelling to read.

For example, let's turn to *Too Shy to Spy* again. In our first plot, he's caught up in an international espionage storyline. He's learning to believe in and rely on himself. We'll want to focus on situations where he's being forced to choose to be confident—the specific setup of his missions, perhaps. As we do this, we must be sure that the character's emotional response isn't the exact same every time. Then, as we're putting these events into our plot, as Alicia Rasley says, "It's best to make every response somehow different, and then assemble them in the order of emotional risk."

So when our character is faced with first simply relaying information for the real spies, he thinks he can do that. Then we work up to the risk gradually. First, our character is roped into acting as backup, then going on a group mission, then striking out on his own in this spy persona. In each situation, he's gradually facing more and more of his fears, his lack of confidence. His emotional responses to each situation will change, of course, as he learns his lesson, but they won't always be "right."

Fail, fail again

Obviously, if our character starts at one extreme (fear, loneliness, naïveté) and goes to the other (courage, love, wisdom), some pretty extreme things must happen in the middle. Most of us don't just wake up one day to have our deepest problems, flaws or hang-ups magically healed. To be believable, this amazing reversal must be prompted by external events.

A single external event isn't enough to demonstrate convincing change. Usually, we'll need a series of causally linked external events—AKA a plot—to yield convincing character change. The character resists the change and continually fails throughout the middle. But as the external events force the character to make real choices, he slowly learns and grows, coming to understand exactly how wrong his emotional starting point was.

Failure yields growth

Throughout the middle of the story, readers see the character striving to maintain his worldview. Keep in mind that this is a long-held belief or habit, deeply ingrained into our character. This behavior was working for the character on some level until the events of the story forced him to grow and change.

It's also okay—advisable, even!—to not build the character arc in a linear way, always incrementally becoming more perfect. In fact, it's more compelling to see the character take two steps forward and one step back. Until that final reversal comes toward the end of our story, the character isn't ready for the change, and he'll do what he can to avoid it.

27

Jason Black, author of the writing blog *Plot to Punctuation*, outlines three phases in this middle section of the novel. At first, the character will fail without understanding why—perhaps she denies the problem exists. Gradually, she begins to understand why she's failing, but she still isn't able to change, because understanding comes only in hindsight. The last, most frustrating phase of the character's arc according to Black is the character being able to see the failure coming, but still feeling powerless to prevent those failures. She feels as though she's incapable of change, that she'll forever be doomed to live in the problematic pre-arc state.

Whenever the character retreats into the pre-arc state, acting from the fears that built her mask in the first place, those choices are going to backfire, hurt her somehow. This failure is part of what prompts her final "growth spurt."

Sometimes, of course, the character will make the right choice in the middle of the story, often by chance or out of desperation. When the character does this, we can use the basic principles of behavioral conditioning to show the character (and the reader) that he's doing the right thing: reward him.

When the character's positive choice brings her closer to the post-arc state, the best "reward" in storytelling terms would be to bring her closer to her external goal. When a negative choice backfires, the biggest "punishment" is to take her farther away from her external goal. It's often best if this reinforcement appears as the natural consequence of the character's choice: she retreats behind her gruff mask and offends her partner, and he withdraws from her, frustrating the love match.

By consistently using this pattern of conditioning, we slowly force the character to see that her pre-arc beliefs and behaviors will no longer work, and she must try something new. Looking over the course of the story (perhaps only subconsciously), she can see the few times those correct actions worked, and the positive outcomes that followed. This positive reinforcement of good choices is all part of building a convincing character arc. Then we force her into an external situation where she has no other choice but to change.

So for our *Too Shy to Spy* hero, when he acts from a place of confidence and courage, the operation he's working on goes well. The team reaches their external goals, or some other positive outcome happens. However, it's difficult for him to overcome his "natural" state, so most of the time, he'll act from his pre-arc place of fear—and when he does, things go wrong. The ops fail, his personal relationships falter, and he gets into even more trouble.

However, as we use conditioning to teach our character the right way to act, we need to make sure she's also facing real choices to ensure that her growth is also real.

Making real choices

To prompt true growth, the choices facing our character must be real, not stacked. Again turning to Alicia Rasley's "Changes and Choices":

> We want to design the events to confront him with choice—and change the events so that each choice he makes is a change away from that initial default res-

> ponse. But there's a danger here. If the choice presented is too stacked in one direction, then it's not a choice. So we can't just present a choice like "help them survive or watch them die." He's not a devil. In a case like that, he will choose the "right" choice—but without any real growth. If every decent human being would make the same choice, it's too easy.

Hopefully, our character isn't a reprehensible human being, so that's not the lesson he needs to learn. This doesn't mean we're descending into a moral quagmire of gray areas with each choice. While the choices might not have a clear-cut "only a reprehensible human would do such a thing" option, there are "right" and "wrong" answers for our character and the story. The "right" choice brings her closer to the final goal of the internal journey; that is, the right choice is the one she would make if she'd already completed the character arc. Gradually, the character comes to realize that retreating into the pre-arc state is a recipe for ultimate failure.

Intermediate turning points

Now that we understand how to execute these important changes, next we must turn to positioning those events in the story. Throughout the middle of the book, there are a number of major milestones in the story's structure that may coincide with the major events of the character arc. While a full discussion of story structure is beyond the scope of this book, here are a few ideas on how to use the specific key milestones of a story's middle section, as outlined in *Story Engineering: Mastering the 6 Core Competencies of Successful Writing* by

Larry Brooks, in the character arc context.

- **First Plot Point** (20-25% mark): "the moment when something enters the story in a manner that affects and alters the hero's status and plans and beliefs, forcing him to take action in response, and thus defining the contextual nature of the hero's experience from that point forward, now with tangible stakes and obvious opposition in place . . . the call for the hero to do something he wasn't doing before" (175).
- Brooks labels this as the most important point of the story, which changes everything. This might be the point at which we fully illustrate how broken the beginning is to launch the character on the external plot and internal journey. To me, the "call for the hero to do something he wasn't before" might indicate that this is the last time his pre-arc state should show any semblance of "working" for him. From here on out, whenever he retreats into his fears, he'll receive negative consequences.

- **First Pinch Point** (37.5% or 3/8s mark): "an example, or a reminder, of the nature and implications of the antagonistic force, that is not filtered by the hero's experience. The reader sees [it] for herself in a direct form" (200).
- As we encounter the antagonistic force, the pinch point is a good time to show the antagonist's parallel or contrasting weakness in action. The antagonist is currently stronger than the protagonist, because the protagonist has yet to complete her journey.

- **Midpoint** (50% mark): "new information that enters the story squarely in the middle of it that changes the *contextual* experience and understanding of either the reader or the hero, or both" (192).

- Here could be a nice place to have the character finally make a good choice in her character journey. She acts in a post-arc way, making the choice that she would after finishing her character arc, whether by chance or desperation, though her inner motivation hasn't changed yet. Or perhaps she actually does have a brief moment of understanding, and she even tries the right action for the right reason. Alternatively, it could constitute a major failure, perhaps if the protagonist *thinks* she's figured out the right way to change, but she's wrong.

- **Second Pinch Point** (62.5% or 5/8s mark): same as the First Pinch Point, "an example, or a reminder, of the nature and implications of the antagonistic force, that is not filtered by the hero's experience. The reader sees [it] for herself in a direct form" (200).
- Again, when we encounter the antagonistic force, this is our opportunity to show the antagonist's alignment with his weakness. By the Second Pinch Point, the protagonist has begun to learn and grow somewhat, but she hasn't learned the lesson fully and hasn't applied it in her life. The antagonist is still stronger because the protagonist needs to continue to grow.

- **Second Plot Point** (75-80% mark): "the final injection of new information into the story, after which no new expository information may enter the story other than the hero's actions, and which puts a final piece of narrative information in play that gives the hero everything she needs to become the primary catalyst in the story's conclusion" (204).

- This might also constitute the last major change along the character's journey, the last clue she'll need when she assembles the evidence later to act from a positive, post-arc state. It could be a positive change toward the post-arc state, or the last major failure in retreating into the pre-arc state. (Blake Snyder opines in *Save the Cat!* that if the Midpoint is positive, the Second Plot Point should be negative, and vice versa.)

These interpretations of the character arc's milestones are suggestions of possible executions—there are many others.

Quite possibly, the beginning, these major milestones, and the climax could be enough to construct a character arc. Character arcs can be built quite subtly. You don't have to overemphasize the character's growth, beating the reader over the head with it. In most stories, the external plot will play a starring role in the story. In fact, the character arc could even qualify as a subplot.

Subplots and secondary characters

Throughout the middle of the novel, we can also use subplots and secondary characters to illustrate the character's internal journey. A subplot is a part of a story that shows some sort of progress, growth, or change, but isn't the main plot of the story (those causally linked external events). By this definition, a character arc meets the criteria of as a subplot. Other subplots often feature secondary characters, i.e., characters other than the main protagonist, antagonist, love interest, etc.

A secondary character can help reinforce the main character's arc by showing the main character a positive example of the post-arc state. A secondary character who already appreciates the lesson the main character is in the process of learning can be yet another piece of evidence the main character needs to understand how she needs to change.

Subplots can also help to shore up and illustrate the character arcs. There are a number of ways to do this, but the two most common are:

- **A mirroring subplot**: A secondary character exhibits the same weakness as the main character, and also embarks on a journey to growth. The secondary character reaps positive consequences. This journey is often less dramatic than the main character's, and it must be different in some way, or it may feel (and possibly be) superfluous.

- **A contrasting subplot**: A secondary character exhibits the same weakness as the main character, but refuses to go on a journey to growth like the main character does. The secondary character reaps negative consequences.

As you develop your subplots, be sure that when the character or secondary character moves in the opposite direction of the character's growth arc, there are always negative consequences. Rewarding a character for acting in the opposite way we'd want our main character to act contradicts the main character's ultimate lesson and undermines the main character arc.

Also, make sure your subplots and secondary characters are necessary. The subplots should intersect with and affect the trajectory of the main character and her arc as well, and the subplots must not overtake the main plot. Likewise, too many secondary characters can easily overwhelm a novel, especially if their purposes are purely comic relief and they don't affect (or worse, undermine) the main character and his internal and external journeys.

External events in action: scene arcs

So far, we've looked at character arcs on a macro level, characters changing over the course of a story. We know that our character's internal changes are best motivated by external plot events, which trigger internal reactions, which, in turn, move the plot forward.

On a smaller scale, the structure of scenes and sequels can help to keep the story and the character arc moving forward. Jack Bickham's book *Scene and Structure* is an excellent resource on learning about this topic.

Bickham's basic scene structure follows the pattern of goal – conflict – disaster.

The goal is the objective of the viewpoint character at the start of the scene, for just that scene. (For a story and a character that feel purposeful and driven, have the character state the goal near the beginning of the scene.) Bickham's conflict is what happens as the character pursues the goal and meets resistance: dialogue, movement, pursuit, etc.

During the conflict section of the scene, the character will be making choices continually: what to say, what to do, how to go

about achieving his goal. These are all opportunities for growing experiences, acting more and more like he should once he's
learned the ultimate lesson of his character journey (or not) and
reaping the consequences on a minute by minute basis.

This conflict builds to the scene's climax, the disaster. This is
generally when the character is working hardest to achieve her
goal, the biggest effort, risk or leap she makes in this scene: the
most important choice. This choice and its consequences are
the biggest opportunities for the character's growth.

To paraphrase Bickham, the goal sets up a question for the
scene in the readers' minds—will the character achieve this?—
and the disaster section answers that question with "Yes,
but . . ," "No," or "No and furthermore . . ." Since we want to
reward the character's positive choices, when he moves toward
the post-arc state, the "answer" at the disaster could be a "Yes,
but . . ." This type of answer means the character achieves his
goal, but it comes with another complication to keep the external plot or internal arc moving forward. When the character
makes a decision that reflects the pre-arc state of fear, his situation gets worse with a "No" or "No, and furthermore . . ."
answer, which not only frustrates the character's external goal
but piles on another problem.

This isn't the only chance the character has for growth. The
second kind of chance—the second kind of *choice*—occurs in a
sequel. The sequel is what follows the scene, the emotional
response. It also has a structure that can help with this kind of
character arc.

Bickham's structure for the sequel is emotion – thought –

decision – action (which leads to another scene). The emotion is the initial response to the events of the scene and its disaster. When the character moves past the initial emotion, she thinks through the events, her response and her options in the thought phase. This ultimately leads to a decision, a choice. By moving through the steps of the sequel, we can lead the character and the reader to create a compelling, convincing choice each time, which ultimately shows convincing *change*.

This choice also sets up the action of the next scene. So the initial goal of the next scene is the result of the character's last sequel. When she's reacting from the pre-arc state, she may choose an action and a goal that aren't in her best interest. Once again, whenever she reverts to a pre-arc state, her choices should ultimately fail.

In our *Too Shy to Spy* example, our hero has been mistaken for an international man of mystery and sent in to meet with a contact. If this is early in the book, he'd be likely to act from a place of fear, so maybe the team of spies he's with have threatened him, or made it clear that he'd be in more danger if he didn't cooperate. Conversely, if he's starting to learn to be confident, he might go in believing he can do accomplish his objectives—or at least that nobody else can do it for him.

Either way, he chooses to undertake the assignment. Note that the choice—the action—is the same despite the motivations here. Because the character arc focuses on his emotions and motivations, the actions themselves often are less important than the reasons he chooses to act.

These reasons, then, help us to figure out what kind of disaster to use in the scene. If our hero is operating from a place of fear, and those fears dominate his choices through the scene, we have a "No" or "No and furthermore . . ." situation. Perhaps the contact doesn't believe he's supposed to meet with our hero (because the hero's confidence falters and he gives himself away somehow). Maybe the contact turns on him and takes him captive.

On the other hand, if our hero is operating from a place of courage and confidence, a "Yes, but . . ." disaster might suit the arc better. He meets the contact, but the contact doesn't have the information he wants. Maybe the contact can even direct the hero to someone who does have the information, but the new mission is even more daunting.

The only time we want to see an uncomplicated "Yes" answer would be at the climax. But first, the character is going to have to get through that final ordeal.

FINISHING: THE CLIMAX, THE ULTIMATE MOMENT OF CHARACTER CHANGE

At the climax of the story, we have to do more than just defeat the external plot forces to provide a satisfying conclusion to our character arc. We either have to show that the character has learned his lesson and can use it to defeat the bad guy, or force the character to make the *big* choice to change, to take a leap of faith into the U-turn, post-arc state.

Show that the character has already learned the lesson

Sometimes, our character has the big epiphany, where he realizes how he needs to change, before the climax. In these situations, the character must show how deeply he learned the lesson by using this new strength to overcome the final obstacle.

Let's say we have a detective who, like all good detectives, thinks she's better off alone. In the middle of the story, she comes to realize and accept that she does, in fact, need help. At the climax, she knows she can't confront the killer alone (because that would be stupid). So she calls in the cavalry to help her and together they defeat the bad guy, proving that the detective learned her lesson and that lesson is right.

If we've tailored our antagonist to match the heroine's weakness, we've probably pitted our detective against an antagonist who insists that he doesn't need anyone else and must do everything himself. At the climax of the story, the detective heroine comes in with her team. While they distract the antagonist, running his operation himself, the detective steals the hostage or other MacGuffin, showing how vital their teamwork is to the effort—while still balancing the need in fiction to have our heroine's actions bring about her success.

One of the biggest things to watch out for with this type of ending is making sure that the character learns her lesson very close to this climax. If these events occur too far apart, the causal link between learning the lesson and the ultimate success at the climax is weakened.

If it's possible to make the final choice in learning the lesson coincide with the climax instead, that helps to prevent the timing problem.

Force the character to take a leap of faith

Another method to bring the character arc to its climax is to force the character to make that final choice, a leap of faith, at the crucial moment. In this type of ending, the character hasn't fully committed to or been convinced of the ultimate change yet. At the climax, he must make the choice to use the lessons he's learned along the way to finally overcome the antagonistic force.

For example, in my forthcoming novel *Bloodstone*, my heroine's journey was one from disbelief to belief. The external plot had to do with bad guys chasing them and a physical confrontation with the main antagonist. In the first draft, the hero and heroine work together to defeat a psycho and the other bad guys. While that's a satisfying conclusion to the external plot, it didn't tie up the internal journey.

I knew it wasn't as good as it could have been. I needed the external and internal plots to hit their high points at the same time. That balance is very difficult. After pondering and brainstorming, I finally found a way to bring those to stories to a head at the same time: I changed the psycho to align him with the heroine's internal journey. At the climax, the antagonist's burgeoning belief falters. He challenges the heroine about what she believes, telling her she's foolish to believe in the hero (who is separated from her right then). Despite the imminent danger, she still chooses to believe and throws her lot in with him instead of compromising—and the hero comes through.

Or, to return to *Too Shy to Spy* again, at the climax, we need our shy hero to drop the spy persona and use his real self, his real capabilities, not hiding behind any other bravado or masks.

Perhaps we can engineer the villain as someone who constantly hides behind other identities. In the end, the hero (as himself) unmasks the villain, which leads directly to the villain's downfall and capture. The hero learns that he's capable and competent and worthy of his own respect, and with this new confidence, he's able to move forward in his life.

With this type of ending, it's vital that the character's growth throughout the story be very clear, so that the final choice at the climax makes sense not only for the external plot but for the character's journey as well.

Putting the pieces together

Both of these climax methods use the same underlying logic. Although there's definitely more than one way to execute a character arc successfully, I've found the following model most helpful in bringing together the pieces of constructing the character arc that we've already discuss to create effective climaxes for my external and internal plots.

To this point, we've established the character's pre-arc state in the broken beginning. We've tailored the antagonist, establishing her as having a weakness that corresponds with the protagonist's (either the same weakness taken to an extreme, or that weakness presented as a strength). We've shown the character gradually coming to understand that their pre-arc state is untenable, and that they must change.

As we come into the climax, the protagonist realizes how he is like the bad guy: they have this same character trait, although the antagonist presents it in a negative way. As our character recognizes that negative element in himself, he realizes how the story events show that this negative element is *not* working in his life—and at the climax, it's *really* not working for the antagonist!

Finally, the character is ready to act upon all these lessons throughout their emotional journey, realizing their ultimate success depends on overcoming their own weakness. We have to bring the character to the moment of the ultimate choice. The whole point of this story, this arc, is forcing the character to *choose*, to willingly leave behind the comfort zone, the mask, and embrace the change, his essence.

Because of what the character has learned and how he's grown—and *only with this knowledge*—he's now strong enough to defeat the antagonist. After all, the antagonist's weakness is that she's exaggerated this flaw, taken it to an extreme, and now our protagonist knows better. As with all our other examples of positive and negative reinforcement, we need to affirm the climactic choice to show that the character has learned her lesson, and that growth is positive. This time, the external reward the character receives is the ultimate victory over the antagonist, and reaching the ultimate goal of the external plot.

As with the previous climax pattern, it's important to time these events as close as possible. Not only does that strengthen the causal link in the minds of readers, but once the character has learned the ultimate lesson, he ceases to grow and change— and be interesting.

If this sounds complex and challenging—it is! But good, worthwhile, effortless reading is the product of concerted writing effort.

An example of the climax in high art: *Kung Fu Panda 2*

I've never seen the movie *Kung Fu Panda*, but the sequel is one of my kids' favorites. The basic premise of *Kung Fu Panda 2* is that Po, the eponymous martial artist panda, realizes that he's adopted. The antagonist, Shen the peacock, is threatening to take over all of China and destroy kung fu.

As we've learned, the wounds and masks that the characters create are often very similar in the antagonist and protagonist. Po's wound is that his biological mother abandoned him. Shen's wound is that, when his parents saw his psychopathic tendencies, they exiled him. Both characters carry a wound because they lost their parents' love.

Through the course of the story, the hero is able to come to grips with the turmoil of his past. He learns to appreciate the friends and family and abilities he has now and find inner peace. With that inner peace, he can harness the full power of kung fu, and he quite literally has the power to defeat the villain's weapon.

The character arcs are even openly stated immediately after Po destroys the weapon:

> SHEN (antagonist): How did you find peace? I took away your parents! Everything! I—I scarred you for life!
>
> PO (protagonist): See, that's the thing, Shen. Scars heal.

> SHEN: No, they don't. Wounds heal!
>
> PO: Oh yeah. What do scars do? They fade, I guess?
>
> SHEN: I don't care what scars do!
>
> PO: You should, Shen. You gotta let go of that stuff from the past 'cause it just doesn't matter! The only thing that matters is what you choose to be now.

The antagonist then makes his choice—to keep doing what he's been doing, to refuse to abandon the mask. Having changed and grown beyond the state where the villain remains stuck, Po taps into his inner peace to draw strength, using his essence. Because of this newfound strength—and only with this—he's able to escape. Po has already foiled the villain's master plan, but in the end, the antagonist's choices destroy him physically as well as emotionally.

Sometimes this principle works on a more metaphorical level, but in *Kung Fu Panda 2* it's quite literal. Because of what the hero has learned on his journey (as prompted by external events), he is now strong enough to defeat not only his own mask and wound, but also to defeat the antagonist, who refuses to grow.

The dénouement

After the climax, we must show the results of the character's final choice to prove that the character has truly changed. Alicia Rasley says, "One last tip—readers will believe in the internal change only if they see it manifested on the external level. So we need some last little event that affirms the choice he made."

In her article "Changes and Choices: External Action and Internal Reaction," Rasley outlines a character journey of a man learning to become part of a family (internal journey) when stranded on a desert island with a teacher and her students (external plot). "Maybe," she says, "the last sight we have of him is [him] surrounded by the kids as they work together move his hut across the stream into the family compound—and Julie [the teacher] helping to set the hut on a new foundation."

We have to show that the character has changed, even if it's a one line postscript. This is important in all stories, but even more critical in stories where the character makes the final leap at the climax to confirm that change is real and permanent, not just an act of momentary convenience to beat the bad guy at a critical juncture.

CHARACTER ARCS
IN RELATIONSHIP STORIES

Relationship stories—romances,
family dramas, "bromances," buddy flicks,
even sports movies—present special
challenges for character arcs.

Relationship stories are all about building a relationship based on love, whether that love is platonic, familial, or romantic. There are lots of ways to do this well, but the following outline helps to not only make sure the internal journeys match up, but that they're integral to the plot (no matter what the external plot is). Plus, it also helps to show that these people in this relationship are "right" for each other—possibly even "perfect."

A relationship story may only have one arcing character. In those cases, it may appear at first that the other member of the relationship also has an arc, such as a parent who *appears* uncaring, but that character will be revealed to be misunderstood somehow.

Multiple arcing characters present a particular challenge Here are a few methods for showing the interplay between the arcs of characters while developing their relationship.

THE PATTERN FOR TRUE LOVE

The essential principles start with the same ideas we discussed from Michael Hauge, as explained by writing craft blogger Jami Gold. To review: first, each character in the main relationship needs his/her own arc. There's something in their lives that's unfulfilled, a need, a void.

Second, each character needs some sort of "wound" in his/her backstory, a painful event that has altered the character's perception of herself/himself and the world.

Third, this wound very much shapes the characters' beliefs about themselves. It leads to them assuming "masks," the way they present themselves to the world. To borrow Hauge's example again, Shrek's wound is that people have always run from him, so he believes he must be terrifying. He assumes the mask of a big, scary ogre to protect himself from going through that kind of rejection again. *Shrek* is all about relationships—with Donkey, with Fiona.

Fourth, the other member of the relationship is eventually able to see past that mask to the character's true "essence," who he truly is or who she truly wants to be. To show their relationship growing, and even make it seem inevitable, every time the characters reveal their true essences to one another (especially willingly), their relationship progresses and they receive trust, understanding or affection.

That is, when they make progress on their character arc, they move closer to one another. Conversely, they'll have problems and conflicts in their relationships when the characters retreat back behind their masks—when they retreat into their comfort zones, their pre-arc states, they pull back from one another.

I've found one more aspect that can make this model particularly powerful in relationship stories. If possible, each character's strength—either one s/he starts with or one s/he acquires through the course of the character arc—should somehow match the wound of their counterpart so that something about each of them heals the other's wound. This also helps fight their mistaken beliefs and defeat their fears to get at their true essences.

Another effective pattern in a relationship story is making the characters each grow and change to become the person the other always needed, reaching their essence to become the perfect fit for their partner. And again, this works in any story in which a relationship is the major focus. A hero and a heroine might learn to trust and commit to one another, while a mother and daughter might learn to accept and understand one another.

We've mentioned before that compelling character arcs are based in internal states that the character can control. A character probably can't change the fact that he's single all by himself (unless he can compel someone to date him by sheer force of will). Rather than simply being lonely or sad at the outset, and having that need filled externally with the arrival of the love interest, the character grows internally. The character's growth is shown, and perhaps he even *becomes* suitable for a relationship with this other character. The romance might be considered an "external" plot here, and because of the internal growth and progress the characters have made, they are able to reach the external goal of finding love.

For an example, in my forthcoming novel *Bloodstone*, the heroine has stopped believing in just about anything. She plays opposite a hero whose wound is that nobody believes in him— everyone laughs in his face whenever he dares to share something very personal. His wound has led him to believe that no one will believe in him, so he must take everything on alone. We've already discussed the individual examples a little, but now we'll combine them to make them even more powerful.

He calls the heroine on her mask (in a big argument!), and later helps her toward her essence, of being a believing person. In turn, she helps him see that he does need help and ultimately he can't go it alone. Together, they're able to show both of their essences—belief and teamwork—in action. Working in tandem, both of their character journeys become more meaningful.

Jane Austen's *Pride and Prejudice* is another good example of these "double character arcs." Mr. Darcy's pride and Elizabeth Bennet's prejudice against him interfere in their relationship. Slowly, Mr. Darcy reveals his true nature, and humbles himself as he helps Elizabeth's sisters despite their low station and sometimes inappropriate behavior. Lizzy, too, learns she was too quick to judge Mr. Darcy, and although she prided herself on her wisdom, she needs to reevaluate the evidence and her previous estimation of Mr. Darcy.

With respect to the external plot, the reader usually needs to see this final change, the characters becoming their true selves for themselves and for one another, at the climax. The characters' fears threaten the relationship, but the characters act on what they've learned throughout their experiences in the story and choose to be brave instead of dominated by their fears, to shed their masks and live in their essences, in order to move forward together.

HERO AS ANTAGONIST: DOUBLE CHARACTER ARCS

Sometimes in romance fiction, and most of its sub-genres, the hero is also an antagonist to the heroine. He's a grump or a tyrant or a renegade. Maybe he's a bitter counter to a sweet and innocent ingénue. The point of the book is for him to understand and accept the heroine, which means the external plot is basically that hero's "villainy" must be "overcome."

The hero has to change—not from actually evil to good, but from rude, inattentive, uninterested or self-absorbed to its opposite. These are not the only options for the hero's role, and the heroine's possible journeys often vary even more. In years past, we often saw the heroine change to fit the hero's standards, lifestyle, etc. But I believe it's more compelling—and acceptable—to have both of them change for themselves and for one another.

I really enjoy the example in the musical *Annie Get Your Gun*—not the original 1946 script (or the 1950 film). The fictionalized story of sharpshooters Frank Butler and Annie Oakley got a much-needed update in Peter Stone's 1999 revival. Frank and Annie both have the same flaw: pride. Neither of them can stand to lose, but when both are part of Buffalo Bill Cody's Wild West troupe, they fall in love despite their ongoing competitiveness.

Their pride continues to get in the way of their romance, however. When Annie upstages Frank's act just before he's about to propose, Frank is so upset that he not only breaks up with her, but he leaves the show altogether. After a long time apart, they reconcile, but their pride interferes once again, and they argue, finally deciding to settle who's the better shot once and for all.

This is where the song "Anything You Can Do, I Can Do Better" comes in, which perfectly sets the tone for their relationship. Secondary characters sabotage Annie's gun, but Frank loans her his. The secondary characters explain to Annie why she has to throw the match to win Frank's heart. After a year apart from the man she loves, Annie decides to sacrifice her pride and misses every shot.

The original version of the musical ended there. The 1999 revival added more to the ending to bring the character arcs' message closer to the 21st century as well. After Annie throws her turn at the match, Frank insists that he take his turn. Knowing what Annie has sacrificed for him (and appreciating that it would be a false victory anyway), Frank also misses every shot, forfeiting his pride, too.

Now that both characters have moved on from their pre-arc states to reveal their true, better natures, they can be together Happily Ever After.

CHARACTER ARCS AND GENDER

Does gender affect character arcs? Of course, absolutely—and not really.

The exact starting and ending points of the character arc should be suited to the character and the story—and gender, of course, will play into who the character is, in the sense that it plays into all of our selves and self-conceptions. However, gender stereotypes, and even scientifically supported observations, are less important to any story or character than who these people are as individuals.

Regardless of gender, the basic pattern will always be the same: start the character at one extreme, lacking something internally; force the character through external events to confront that lack and try new ways to alleviate it; and finally come to the reversal (and prove the change) at the climax and/or conclusion, where the character is now at the other extreme.

But the exact characteristics that she'll change or the exact events that will make him grow will vary depending on the character and the story. While these may be somewhat dictated by gender—most of the time, you're not going to see a woman in a romance be the one to confront her own commitment issues, for example—at its heart, the character arc pattern is universal, and rooted in the ways that real people grow and change, no matter their gender, race, ethnicity, or other factors. That's part of the reason why the internal journey is so powerful in fiction. Character arcs are especially vital to relationship stories, making the ultimate relationship fulfilling for the characters and readers alike.

Non-growth Character Arcs

Not all characters grow and change
in a positive way. There are several
non-growth character arc patterns,
including negative arcs, flat arcs,
and none whatsoever.

THE NEGATIVE CHARACTER ARC

Not all changes shown in fiction are positive. Negative changes, or waiting too long to make positive changes, are hallmarks of tragedies. Both of these arcs are rewarded with negative consequences.

The broken (or unsettling) beginning

"Something is rotten in the state of Denmark," as Marcellus observes in Act I of Shakespeare's *Hamlet*. In the opening of a tragedy, something is often not quite right. It might not be as dramatic as the king's ghost, or the thunder and lightning that accompany the three witches of *Macbeth*, but there is some hint that something is truly wrong with this world, especially for our hero.

Typically, tragic heroes suffer from a fatal flaw. Aristotle taught that a good tragic hero evokes a sense of pity or fear from the audience, and that flaw is the source. Macbeth goes from loyal to disloyal and murderous because of his flaw: pride. In his typical arc, he resists the change at first, but repeated urging and external events prompt him to his downward spiral. After the witches leave the stage, Macbeth arrives victorious from battle, greeted by friends who predict he'll be the next king. Macbeth is stunned into silence, setting up an unsettling start to his character journey.

It's downhill from there.

The worsening middle

Throughout the middle of the story, the tragic hero is presented with real choices, just like the hero of a growth arc. However, unlike the hero who evolves, the tragic hero either refuses to change, or actually chooses the worse path, the option sure to hurt someone.

Again, real choices make a real difference here. If the character is presented with stacked choices toward the negative ("If you don't kill King Duncan, I'll murder your children slowly."), he's simply acting out of self-preservation or protection of loved ones, rather than degenerating, and he doesn't deserve the tragic ending.

With each choice, the character should be presented with a better option, one that gives him a chance to come back from this dark place. But the character remains focused on his ultimate goal at all costs, bringing him to the point of no return.

The tragic climax

Finally, the tragic hero is brought to a point where he must make a leap. He makes the biggest choice that seems to bring him to his final goal. This choice becomes the point of no return. The character has now sacrificed so much or committed so great a crime that she cannot go back to who she was at the outset of the story.

Macbeth makes his irrevocable choice when he murders the king. However, that's just the beginning of the climactic sequence of a tragedy. The irreversible action comes with negative consequences, beyond just the immense guilt Macbeth and Lady Macbeth carry. The murder sets the ultimate climax of the external plot into action to bring the hero to justice for his failure to correct his flaw, and Macbeth himself is killed.

The change delayed

Another popular pattern for a negative arc is a positive change made too late. The basic change in Shakespeare's *Hamlet* is positive: Hamlet learns to take action to avenge his father's murder. His is, at heart, indecisive, someone who does not act. The external events of the play give him plenty of opportunities to take action.

Instead, he spends the entire play delaying this change in his character, debating and dithering. When he finally does act in the climactic sequence, his love interest, Ophelia; her father, royal counselor Polonius; and others have already died. These avoidable tragedies incite Laertes, Polonius's son, to a plan of vengeance, which ends with just about everybody dying, and the Kingdom of Denmark falling to Norway. Negative consequences for sure.

If you're striving to write a tragedy, delay a positive change past the point of necessary action, or bring the character from a positive state to a negative one.

THE FLAT CHARACTER ARC

The typical pattern of character arcs doesn't quite work for a character who is already good in whatever respect the story is focusing on. Sometimes the story is not a journey to improvement, but a proving ground of something the character has already learned.

The good beginning

In a flat character arc, we must show the character's starting point as good. This can be challenging because it's very hard for readers to sympathize with someone who comes off as perfect. To establish a character as strong without sacrificing reader sympathy, be sure to include some struggles, either in other areas of her life, or perhaps some temptation in holding true to lessons he's already learned.

These temptations become even stronger as the story progresses.

The tempting middle

With this type of character arc, the most vital thing to remember is that the character must truly be tempted. If the character has no moral dilemma, nothing worth changing for, never even considers altering, there's little conflict, and even less compelling the reader to read. Instead, we must make it difficult for him to maintain his goodness. As C.S. Lewis says:

> No man knows how bad he is till he has tried very hard to be good. A silly idea is current that good people do not know what temptation means. This is an obvious lie. Only those who try to resist temptation know how strong it is. After all, you find out the strength of the German army by fighting against it, not by giving in. You find out the strength of a wind by trying to walk against it, not by lying down. A man who gives in to temptation after five minutes simply does not know what it would have been like an hour later. (*Mere Christianity*, 134.)

62

Thus the character proves how truly good he is by continuing to fight as it becomes increasingly difficult to remain true to his previous lessons. Unlike in a growth arc, the character is not necessarily rewarded for making the correct choices, making it even more difficult for him to choose right.

The consequences of these correct choices often grow worse throughout the middle of the story, and the temptation greater. As we approach the climax, it's often most effective to try to persuade the character (and the reader) that there would be no negative consequences to giving in and living by convenience, taking the path of least resistance.

But the character's troubles are far from over.

The ending: fairy tale or tragedy

At the climax of the story, the flat-arc hero must face the final temptation. Here, the hero might meet a reward for her long-suffering. A character who remains good throughout a story despite temptation is a familiar pattern in fairy tales: the perennially good Cinderella befriends the animals who help her to overcome the villainess.

Alternatively, these stories may end in tragedy. For example, in *A Man for All Seasons*, Sir Thomas More already has the moral high ground. He will not bow to Henry VIII's choice to break with the pope because he knows the king is motivated not by religious principles but by a desire to divorce his wife. The story shows More's goodness: he's willing to sacrifice his life for his moral convictions—and he does.

THE NON-ARCING CHARACTER

So are character arcs required? The answer, of course, is it depends—and it depends on several factors.

In plot-driven fiction, for example, the character's growth and change often aren't the focus or purpose of the story. Dirk Pitt, James Bond, and Indiana Jones see little, if any, character growth in each episode of their stories (aside from the new Bond movies, maybe). While they are memorable characters, and we root for them to win, we don't care if they have a life-altering experience to become better people. We're cool with them staying the way they are. The story focuses on their adventures rather than their experiences.

However, in character-driven fiction, and especially in literature where we are able to share so much more of a character's inner life, the character arc is central. This kind of fiction enables readers to live the character's experiences and feelings, and those are at least as important to the story as the actual actions.

Genre can influence the use of a character arc. Mysteries and action stories tend to be more plot driven, i.e., headed toward a pre-determined ending point where the villain is punished, though character arcs are still helpful in creating a richer character and a richer experience for the reader. Romances, especially at single-title length, are usually more driven by the character's internal growth needed to achieve a plot-oriented outcome: the Happily Ever After. The adventure genre, on the other hand, seems particularly suited to the non-arcing character.

The character himself is another important feature in determining whether or not he needs an arc. A non-arcing character usually already comes with talents, strengths, and foibles which readers come to know and love. (How does Bond take his martini or introduce himself? How does Indiana Jones feel about snakes or historical artifacts?)

Another consideration is whether the book will lead into a series and if so, whether the series has a predetermined length and endpoint, or is more open-ended. If this is going to be a serial character, how many different lessons can she learn? It's possible, of course, to do a metaarc—one that takes the character on a journey from the beginning to the end of the series (Harry Potter?)—but it will probably require considerable planning.

If a character arc simply isn't right for your character and your story, take care to *not* set up an arc in the beginning. Avoid anything that might resemble an illustrating incident, and don't give your character any apparent emotional weaknesses that look like they'll be resolved in the course of the story. He might still show imperfection, but avoid showing any negative consequences in an illustrating incident until later in the work.

REVISING CHARACTER ARCS
FOR MAXIMUM IMPACT

Whether or not we design our character arcs
from the beginning and engineer events
to bring about the change,
revision is useful to our character arcs.

Not all of us plan our character arcs in advance, design the plot around the desired changes, and come out with a pretty strong basis for our character arc after prewriting and the first draft. Maybe we changed our character's arc in the middle of the book (or didn't even find it until then!). Perhaps we didn't even start to think about a character arc until we reached the revision stage.

Yes, it's okay to find or develop or change your character arc after you write the book. Sometimes it's easiest that way: you see what your character learned and then go back to the beginning to make it match the conclusion better.

REDISCOVERING YOUR CHARACTER'S ARC

Whether you planned your character's arc from the early phases of prewriting or discovered it only after a draft or two, the first step of revising that arc is to revisit its overall structure, first in the story's two endpoints, then throughout the middle.

Beginning and ending

If you haven't planned out a character arc in advance, the beginning and ending are the best places to start. With a completed book, typically either the beginning or the end of the character arc is in place, so the other might require more work.

In a guest post on the blog *Writer Unboxed*, A. Victoria Mixon talks about rethinking your character arcs and motivations after the first draft, starting with the end of the book:

What is this protagonist's primary overwhelming need? I know we wrote this down way back in the beginning and stuck it up on post-it notes over our desk (you didn't?), but I want to ignore that at this point, and we'll apply ourselves solely to the protagonist in the Climax that we so recently and brilliantly wrote. . . .

Now, what deep inside this protagonist is pitted against them in that Climax? Not external forces—internal. What do they love and believe that's irreconcilable with their first need? What's the equal-but-opposite fire in their belly in this Climactic scene that's fighting back?

Remember to focus only upon the climax scene of the Climax. . . .

Now we'll ask ourselves, "Exactly how could these two needs have gotten this protagonist into this dreadful calamity?"

If that's a little too theoretical, let's look back at how we dis-covered our character arc in the first place. We can turn to the beginning or the end of the novel and look at the state of your character. If you know what lesson the character must learn from the outset, we must make sure she gets there. Conversely, if we know how the character has grown or changed from the events of the novel, we need to make sure we set him up in the opposite position.

If both are in place, we're doing good!

Revision checklist for character arc beginnings

- ☐ The character's emotional starting point:
    - ☐ Suits the character's emotional ending point.
    - ☐ Is negative.
    - ☐ Is shown in the illustrating incident.
    - ☐ Has a negative consequence in the illustrating incident.
- ☐ The character's negative starting point reflects an internal state that they have enough control over to change.
- ☐ The character exhibits both strengths and struggles (maintaining sympathy).

Revision checklist for character arc endings

- ☐ The character's emotional ending point:
    - ☐ Suits the character's emotional start point.
    - ☐ Is positive.
    - ☐ Is shown in the dénouement in a positive light.

Middles

Throughout the middle of the narrative, we want to balance the external actions of the story and the character's internal growth to show the change in a realistic way.

As we established in the last chapter, the external actions of the story—the plot—help to illustrate the character's internal growth by forcing her to make real choices. Throughout the middle, the character will often make the wrong choice (or perhaps the right choice for the wrong reasons) because she's acting from the same beliefs she held at the beginning of the story.

When the character makes the wrong choice, the consequences

must be negative so that the character can learn not to do that again! The negative consequences will usually mean that the character gets farther away from his internal or external goal.

The character's responses to the various events should not all be the same. He should try to change his responses, varying them to try to get to his end goal. It's generally a good idea to order these responses roughly from smallest emotional risk to largest as we approach the climax. This may include reordering events of the plot, or changing the character's responses to those events.

Revision checklist for middles

- ☐ The external events of the plot present the character with real choices (not stacked choices).
- ☐ The character chooses the "wrong" alternative at least some of the time, reacting from the pre-arc state.
- ☐ When the character chooses wrong, there are negative consequences, taking the character farther from the ultimate goal.
- ☐ The character's choices and reactions are varied, not repetitive, throughout the middle.
- ☐ The choices the character faces are arranged to progressively challenge him more and more, forcing greater emotional risks as the story progresses.

Subplots and secondary characters

Not all stories require many subplots or secondary characters. Done ineffectively, secondary characters and subplots can detract from your main characters, their external plot, and their character arcs. So if you use these elements, be sure they're helping your story and your character arcs to the greatest effect.

Effective secondary characters and their subplots are integral to the story. They impact the world around them, especially the main character and her life. As you weave in subplots and secondary characters, look for more places for them to interact with the main character's external and internal journeys. Can they help—or hinder!—her growth? Can they bring about or otherwise influence the external events of the plot?

To make them an even more vital part of the story, you can use subplots and secondary characters to reinforce the main character's internal journey, by either mirroring or contrasting it. But make sure they're not undermining that journey.

Revision checklist for secondary characters and subplots

☐ The secondary characters impact the main character or the external storyline: at least one of their choices alters the course of the book, or influences the main character and his/her decisions.

☐ The subplots do not upstage or overwhelm the main plot: they're not more dramatic or interesting, and they don't get more page time.

Revision checklist for a mirroring subplot

☐ The secondary character's weakness is the same or highly similar to the main character's.

☐ The secondary character's internal journey is still unique, and doesn't simply repeat the main character's.

☐ The secondary character's plot is not more interesting or dramatic than the main character's.

☐ Like the main character, when the secondary character makes a positive choice that moves him toward his improved end state, he is rewarded, reaching his external goals on some level.

☐ The ultimate outcome of the character's journey is positive. She doesn't necessarily have to attain all her goals, but we need to see her changed state as an improvement.

Revision checklist for a contrasting subplot

☐ The secondary character's weakness is the same as or highly similar to the main character's.

☐ The secondary character does *not* go on a journey to growth.

☐ When the secondary character refuses to grow, she reaps negative consequences.

☐ The ultimate outcome for the character is negative.

Climaxes

The climax of the story is the real crux of the lesson our character learns, where she has to take the final leap of faith and apply the nascent understanding she's begun to develop throughout the events of the middle.

As we mentioned before, the character's arc must be vital to her ultimate victory here. She must take what she's learned through the external events of the story (pre-arc state = bad; post-arc state = good) and apply these lessons. Using this new-found strength—and only *with* this newfound strength—the character is now able to defeat the antagonist.

The character may learn the lesson just before the climax of the external plot and apply that lesson, or he may come to the final conclusion during the external plot climax and choose the "right" option to reach not only the post-arc state but also the ultimate victory in the external plot.

Just like the emotional starting point at beginning of the novel, the emotional ending point must be demonstrated on "screen," even if it's just a small action in the dénouement.

Revision checklist for the climax and dénouements

- ☐ The character learns the final lesson immediately before or during the external actions of the climax.
- ☐ The character must take a risk, make a leap of faith, to act in the post-arc state—and be rewarded.
- ☐ The character's emotional ending point:
  - ☐ Mirrors the character's emotional starting point.
  - ☐ Is an improvement over the previous state (in growth arcs).
  - ☐ Is necessary for the ultimate victory at the climax.
- ☐ The final, post-arc state is shown in a positive light in the dénouement.

REVISING CHARACTER ARCS IN RELATIONSHIP STORIES

Relationship stories present a few special challenges in addition to those outlined above. The themes of the arcs as well as the timing should be intertwined to create the maximum effect.

Revision checklist for relationship stories with one arcing character

- ☐ Only one character is shown to need an emotional journey in the illustrating incident. (It may *appear* at first that the other member of the relationship also has an arc, such as a parent who appears uncaring but will be revealed to be misunderstood.)

☐ When the arcing character makes progress toward her post-arc state, she also grows closer to the non-arcing character in the relationship.

☐ Throughout the story and/or in the conclusion, any misunderstood character is shown to have a valid reason for *not* changing. (Often this is the journey of the main character to accepting their partner for who they are.)

Revision checklist for relationship stories with multiple arcing characters

☐ Each character in the story shows their emotional starting point in an illustrating incident. These incidents may coincide, or they may have separate incidents.

☐ The characters present "masks" to each other, not revealing their true "essences" at the outset.

☐ As the characters move toward their essences, their post-arc states, their relationship improves, and they receive trust, understanding or affection.

☐ If possible, the characters' strengths—one they each start with or one they acquire through the course of the character arc—should somehow match their partner's weakness, so that something about each character heals the other's wound, helps him to shed his mask, helps her to become the person she was always meant to be (her essence).

☐ The characters' arcs reach their climax simultaneously, or nearly so. The fears that so dominated their life and determined their worldviews again threaten their relationship, but they choose to live in their essences instead, for themselves and for one another.

☐ The most meaningful changes in relationship stories are made by the characters to improve themselves, and not solely to appease the other person.

REVISING NON-GROWTH CHARACTER ARCS

In tragedies and other stories where the character doesn't show positive growth, the requirements are slightly different. A character with a negative or flat arc must start out in a positive position and follow the patterns for their stories, while a nonarcing character must not set up an emotional journey which he then fails to take.

Revision checklist for negative character arcs

☐ The opening of the story foreshadows its tragic ending with a beginning that's unsettling somehow.

☐ The main character begins in a positive or strong position, which may be shown in an illustrating incident.

☐ The main character also exhibits a tragic flaw, which may lead him to make poor choices.

☐ The main character is given opportunities to make a positive choice, but he doesn't.

☐ The opportunities to change for the better present real choices, not alternatives stacked only toward the negative.

☐ Ultimately, the character makes an irreversible commitment to his negative arc, enacting the climactic sequence.

☐ In the climactic sequence and the finale, the character meets his unfortunate fate, a natural consequence of the good that he's betrayed.

Revision checklist for a flat character arc

☐ The main character already possesses a positive trait which is shown in the character's illustrating incident.

☐ Despite showing this strength, the character still maintains reader sympathy by displaying struggles.

☐ Throughout the middle of the story, the character truly struggles to maintain his positive trait through increasingly tempting experiences.

☐ At the end, the character is faced with the ultimate consequences of maintaining this positive trait:

    ☐ In a positive or fairy-tale type ending, the character ultimately triumphs, often with help. (In many fairy tales, this help may be supernatural.)

    ☐ In a negative or tragic ending, the character's triumph is only moral as he pays the ultimate price for remaining true to the good in him. (In many tragedies, the character may sacrifice his life.)

Revision checklist for a non-arcing character

☐ The beginning of the story does *not* set up a character journey. The character does *not* have an obvious emotional or internal weakness which will be resolved in the course of the story.

    ☐ If the character does show an imperfection, avoid an apparent illustrating event: do not show negative consequences immediately thereafter, especially during the opening chapters.

☐ The character exhibits a larger-than-life quality.

☐ The character may embark on an adventure that's larger-than-life in some way. (Even a small-town murder mystery can have that extraordinary quality.)

☐ The character has traits and foibles the reader can

remember them by. In a way, these familiarities substitute for growing with the character.

☐ The story may focus more on the external plot than the character's internal states and reactions.

☐ If you anticipate writing a series, plan character arcs for future volumes, or avoid them from the outset. A character who learns and grows may be more compelling, but it's also more difficult to find new lessons as a series progresses.

SPECIAL CONSIDERATIONS WITH CHARACTER ARCS

Character arcs are useful for almost all stories. But will they work for all characters, especially for those don't narrate the journey? And what about when those external goals change or are frustrated?

Arcs for Non-Viewpoint Characters

Character arcs are generally easiest to portray through the eyes of the person changing, whether in first person or third person perspective. However, sometimes we need to see a change in a character who isn't a viewpoint character, i.e., the character does not narrate scenes.

When it's a non-viewpoint character arcing, we'll have to work even harder to *show* the change, and have the character verbalize their feelings, reactions, and observations with respect to the situation more. As with traditional character arcs, we must show the pre-arc state in an illustrating incident where our viewpoint character gets to participate in some way—if the non-viewpoint character just tells us about it later, it isn't *shown*, and the reader impact is dramatically reduced.

Throughout the non-viewpoint character's arc, we must take special care to keep the external events occurring on the page, so the reader can observe as much as possible. Unless he's a main character—such as the hero in a romance—he doesn't need as many external events as a main viewpoint character might.

A non-viewpoint character's arc is a good way to help characterize the main character and show his change. Be sure not to squander that opportunity, or to make your main character appear judgmental. If the arc is a positive one, our character might admire the foil character for changing. Or, if our viewpoint character isn't yet ready to change, she might resent the other character's flexibility.

Secondary characters' arcs are better suited to this method, where the changes are generally less dramatic and less integral to the story. Before you use this method for a main character, ask yourself if the story would be stronger if you included the arcing character's viewpoint. When a main character has an arc, but not a perspective, it's not only more difficult to show the arc, but the arc will also have less of an impact.

THE UNEXPECTED TWIST

The Rolling Stones teach us, "You can't always get what you want." Our characters can't, either. Sometimes the goals they start out with at the beginning of the story never come to pass—the external goal, that is. When the character learns and grows through a character arc, you can still create a coherent, fulfilling story when the character's external goal changes or disappoints.

The character's goal at the outset of the story might reflect the pre-arc state. Blinded by fears, he sets his sights lower than he should. The hero of *Too Shy to Spy* might start off only wanting to ask a woman on a date. Instead, as he discovers his confidence, he might fall in love with a female spy (and learn to keep up with her!). In the conclusion, the reader needs to see his confidence demonstrated. That may not be by asking out the same woman from our illustrating incident—but as long as he's obviously confident enough to ask a woman out, the reader can be satisfied.

The character's external goal might change. A doctor seeking for others' approval gains confidence. Perhaps he no longer needs the AMA's endorsement to feel validated in his work. A person seeking to exact revenge learns the meaning of justice. The reality show entrant discovers her prize doesn't bring her the emotional change she really needs.

On the surface, that might sound like a pretty cruddy story. "A woman risks her life on a reality TV show only to discover that the prize does her no good" or "A doctor seeks AMA's golden seal, then decides he doesn't need it." But when the readers dig into the growth and changes, they still get to experience the fulfillment of a goal—albeit one that isn't conscious at the outset.

If you're planning a twist ending where your reader doesn't get his initial goal, be sure the character arc is as strong as possible to avoid disappointing your readers. The character's internal journey makes the story far more compelling and won't leave your readers feeling unfulfilled.

Concluding on Character Arcs

Character arcs are challenging, and sometimes we leave them to chance. But if we execute our character arcs well, they make our fiction fulfilling to our characters—and our readers.

Character arcs are vital in most fiction. We read to connect with people emotionally as they grow and change on the journey. The transformative nature of character arcs has been a significant part of fiction since long before Aristotle coined the term "catharsis" for any extreme change in emotion that results in renewal and restoration. Watching that transformation, rooting for it, and growing with the character are major reasons we read fiction.

In my opinion, a good character arc transcends genre and subject material. While the external events of the plot will usually be what capture readers' attention and keep them turning pages, even a subtle character arc can imbue a book which might otherwise be a "fluffy beach read" with lasting resonance.

REFERENCES

WORKS CITED

Bickham, Jack M. *Scene and Structure*. Cincinnati, OH: Writer's Digest, 1993.

Black, Jason. "Show Some Character! -- Five Steps to Building a Believable Character Arc." *PlotToPunctuation.com*. 20 May 2010.
<http://www.plottopunctuation.com/blog/show/81>.

Brooks, Larry. *Story Engineering: Mastering the 6 Core Competencies of Successful Writing*. Cincinnati, OH: Writer's Digest, 2011

Gold, Jami. "Michael Hauge's Workshop: Are These Characters the Perfect Match?" *Jami Gold Paranormal Author*. 14 Aug. 2012. <http://jamigold.com/2012/08/michael-hauges-workshop-are-these-characters-the-perfect-match/>.

Hauge, Michael. *Writing Screenplays That Sell*. New York, NY: HarperPerennial, 1991.

Lewis, C. S. *Mere Christianity*. London: Fount, 1997.

Mixon, A. Victoria. "Rethinking Motivation for Character Arc."

Writer Unboxed. 8 Oct. 2011.
<http://writerunboxed.com/2011/10/08/darecomplete/>.

Rasley, Alicia. "Changes and Choices: External Action and Internal Reaction." *AliciaRasley.com.*
<http://www.aliciarasley.com/artchanges.htm>.

Snyder, Blake. *Save the Cat!: The Last Book on Screenwriting You'll Ever Need.* Studio City, CA: M. Wiese Productions, 2005.

EXAMPLES CITED

—. *Too Shy to Spy.* Nonexistent novel.

Annie Get Your Gun. By Dorothy Fields, Herbert Fields, and Peter Stone. Eccles Stage Outdoor Amphitheater, Sundance, Utah. 16 Aug. 2013. Performance.

Austen, Jane. *Pride and Prejudice.*

Bolt, Robert. *A Man for All Seasons.* London: Heinemann, 1960.

Kung Fu Panda 2. Dir. Jennifer Yuh Nelson. Perf. Jack Black and Gary Oldman. DreamWorks, 2011.

McCollum, Jordan. *Bloodstone.* Pleasant Grove, Utah: Durham Crest Books, forthcoming.

McCollum, Jordan. *I, Spy.* Pleasant Grove, Utah: Durham Crest Books, 2013

REFERENCES

Shakespeare, William. *Hamlet.*

Shakespeare, William. *Macbeth.*

Shrek. Dir. Andrew Adamson and Vicky Jenson. Perf. Mike Myers, Eddie Murphy and Cameron Diaz. Paramount Home Entertainment, 2007.

True Lies. Dir. James Cameron. Perf. Arnold Schwarzenegger and Jamie Lee Curtis. Twentieth Century Fox, 1994.

FURTHER READING

A few selected resources I think are especially helpful in understanding character arcs.

Campbell, Joseph. *The Hero with a Thousand Faces.* Princeton, NJ: Princeton UP, 1968.

Gold, Jami. "Michael Hauge's Workshop: An Antidote to 'Love at First Sight'." *Jami Gold Paranormal Author.* 9 Aug. 2012. <http://jamigold.com/2012/08/michael-hauges-workshop-an-antidote-to-love-at-first-sight/>.

Gold, Jami. "Michael Hauge's Workshop: Combining Emotional Journeys and External Plots." *Jami Gold Paranormal Author.* 21 Aug. 2012. <http://jamigold.com/2012/08/michael-hauges-workshop-making-emotional-journeys-and-external-plots-play-together/>.

Hardy, Janice. "Defining Story Arcs." *The Other Side of the Story*. 6 July 2011. <http://blog.janicehardy.com/2009/09/re-write-wednesday-arc-enemy.html>.

Hardy, Janice. "Grow Up Already: Character Arcs and Plot." *The Other Side of the Story*. 21 Jan. 2011. <http://blog.janicehardy.com/2011/01/find-your-plot-friday-grow-up-already.html>.

Hardy, Janice. "The Inner Struggle: Guides for Using Inner Conflict That Make Sense." *The Other Side of the Story*. 20 Aug. 2012. <http://blog.janicehardy.com/2012/08/the-inner-struggle-guides-for-using.html>.

Hardy, Janice. "Why Character Arcs (and Growth) Make Readers Care." *The Other Side of the Story*. 25 Feb. 2013. <http://blog.janicehardy.com/2013/02/why-character-arcs-and-growth-make.html>.

Mystery Man on Film (Pseudonymous). "Character Arcs." *Mystery Man on Film*. 14 June 2007. <http://mysterymanonfilm.blogspot.com/2007/06/character-arcs.html>.

Mystery Man on Film (Pseudonymous). "On Character Arcs." *Mystery Man on Film*. 18 Oct. 2006. <http://mysterymanonfilm.blogspot.com/2006/10/on-character-arcs.html>. On "flat" character arcs.

Rasley, Alicia. "The Internal Journey." *AliciaRasley.com*.

<http://www.aliciarasley.com/artinternal.htm>.

Sicoe, Veronica. "The 3 Types of Character Arc – Change, Growth and Fall." *Veronica Sicoe.* 29 Apr. 2013. <http://www.veronicasicoe.com/blog/2013/04/the-3-types-of-character-arc-change-growth-and-fall/>.

Unknown "Unk" Screenwriter (Pseudonymous). "Transformational Character Arcs." *PDF.* 2007. <http://files.meetup.com/184318/Transformational-Character-Arc-series.pdf>.

Vogler, Christopher. *The Writer's Journey: Mythic Structure for Writers.* Studio City, CA: M. Wiese Productions, 1998.

Index

THANK YOU FOR READING!

If you enjoyed this book,
please tell your writing friends & review it online.

To sign up for information on upcoming releases, please visit
http://JordanMcCollum.com/newsletter/

Find character arc worksheets and graphics at my website:
http://JordanMcCollum.com/books/character-arcs/

WRITING CRAFT CLASSES!

I'm now offering classes on writing craft through my website! Topics include character depth, character arcs, structural self-editing and more!

Class sizes are kept small to feature personal interaction and hand-on help. Lesson materials go beyond an overview of the topics presented to dig into how to apply those techniques in your current work.

Be sure to join my mailing list to be the first to hear about future class schedules and topics!

http://JordanMcCollum.com/newsletter/

Writing Craft Series

Character Sympathy

Out now

Whether your character is an angel or a devil, your readers need to be onboard to want to read on. Create character sympathy to draw your readers in and get them rooting for your character.

Tension, Suspense & Surprise

Coming soon

What keeps a reader glued to your novel no matter what the hour? Tension and suspense. Blend these techniques with surprise to keep your readers turning those pages in any genre.

Character Depth

Coming soon

Is your character—and your plot—coming off one-dimensional? Your characters don't have to be philosophers to be "deep." Make your characters come to life and give your readers the immersive emotional experience they crave.

ACKNOWLEDGMENTS

With every book I write, I learn once again that there's no way I could pursue this dream alone.

As always, my family was an amazing support during the production of this book. My husband Ryan did the dishes, listened to me rant about how overburdened I was, and so much more to keep me sane and help me get this book completed. My adorable children, Hayden, Rebecca, Rachel and Hazel, were very patient with their mom, even when she was too stressed to do them the same courtesy. My parents, Ben and Diana Franklin, and my sisters, Jaime, Brooke and Jasmine, have been a support to me throughout my life. My wonderful critique partners, Julie Coulter Bellon and Emily Gray Clawson, provided encouragement and cheering on whenever I needed.

I'm grateful to everyone who attended my class on character arcs at the 2013 LDStorymakers Conference, even (or perhaps especially) those whose questions I couldn't answer. I hope I've addressed all your questions here. The positive responses to the class and to my blog posts on the topic inspired me to expand my thoughts and try to find a wider audience to share with.

I must defer to the expertise of others for some of my literary analysis in this book, especially my mother, Diana Franklin, and my best friend, Sarah Anderson. My beta readers, Mel Hughes, Savita Narayan, Marie Cecelia Austin and Tonette dela Luna, took time and care to edit this book and provide me with much needed feedback. I was thrilled to have Janice Hardy accept my invitation to write a foreword, and floored by her kind words. Becca Puglisi also provided invaluable help in the process of writing this book.

Most of all, I'm grateful to the wonderful authors and bloggers who have helped me learn more about the craft of writing, giving me the tools to process the nuances of storytelling so I could eventually share some of that knowledge. Special credit must go to Larry Brooks, Jami Gold, Janice Hardy, and Alicia Rasley and Theresa Stevens, all of whom selflessly share their expertise on their blogs and websites, and who have been extremely kind to me personally.

ABOUT THE AUTHOR

PHOTO BY JAREN WILKEY

An award-winning fiction author, Jordan McCollum enjoys teaching through her writing craft blog at JordanMcCollum.com, as the Education Director of Authors Incognito (an online writers' support group with over four hundred members), and in her Writing Craft series. On the fiction side, she is the author of the romantic suspense novels *I, Spy* and *Spy for a Spy* in the Spy Another Day series. She makes her home in Utah with her husband and their four children.

Made in the USA
Lexington, KY
24 December 2014